ACTS OF FAITH 2

Dramas for
God's People

Pentecost

BRAD KINDALL

Joy Resources

ACTS OF FAITH 2
Dramas for God's People
Pentecost

Contributing editor: Catherine Malotky

Editors: Scott Tunseth, James Satter

Cover and text design: James Satter

ISBN 0-8066-4494-X

The paper used in this publication meets the minimum requirements of American National Standard for Information Sciences—Permanence of Paper for Printed Library Materials, ANSI Z329.48-1984.

Manufactured in the U.S.A.

06   05   04   03   02   1   2   3   4   5   6   7   8   9   10

Contents

Foreword
The Power of Drama

Seeing is believing . . . Seeing is experiencing . . . Seeing is remembering. Stories have the power to help us believe, experience, and remember because stories help us "see." That's why Jesus spoke in parables. Because stories help us see with our hearts the kindness of God.

Drama is form of storytelling. Like the parables of Jesus, dramas help us see, experience, and remember the message. As Brad Kindall, the principal author of the dramas in this collection, says, the question in designing worship is not, "How do we say it?" but rather "How do we help them see it?" Dramas have the power to convey truth because they:

- *Visualize* the message—they help us "see" the message lived out, acted out, and put into a real context.

- *Imagine* the message—rather than hitting us between the eyes, the drama message comes to us subtly, it sneaks up on us from the side rather than from the front, drawing us in by capturing our imaginations and surprising us with truth.

Dramas move the message of the worship and sermon experience to the heart. The dramas in this collection come out of the worship experience of Community Church of Joy. Each drama was developed out of a team planning process that looks at the entire service as the message and then creates the storyline of that message using music, the sermon, video clips, dance occasion, and drama.

In some cases, the drama serves to set up the question with which the sermon will be dealing. In other cases the drama is self contained, setting up the situation and bringing it to conclusion to reinforce the point of the service and sermon. In all cases, the drama helps people see, experience, and remember the message of the service.

Though created for the worship experience, these dramas can also be used at retreats, in seminars, at banquets, and at other church events. We hope you enjoy these dramas and find them useful in your setting as you seek to help people believe, experience, and remember the kindness of God as seen in Jesus.

TIM WRIGHT
Executive Pastor and Performing Arts Coach
Community Church of Joy
Glendale, Arizona

Introduction

Using drama in the church has a long tradition in human history. For the ancient Greeks, it could even be said that drama *was* church. The great Greek dramatists were the theologians of their day, exploring their gods' interaction with human beings and the nature of life as a human community. Medieval Christian churches used dramas regularly to declare the stories of the Bible and to explore the issues behind them. Because very few people couldn't read at that time, drama was a common way to teach.

Today, when film, video games, computers, and TV have so much influenced on our lives, drama remains a powerful way to invite people to think in new ways. Drama is storytelling. It can be more engaging than a more static expository reading or telling because it taps into our emotions, making it more memorable.

The good news is that it doesn't take too much to do it well enough. For several practical suggestions, see the section "Beginning comments for the director" on page 8.

Use these dramas any time (including retreats and Bible studies), but be sure to try them in worship. Generally, they will be linked closely to preaching. They are responses to Scripture. Sometimes they are the antithesis of the themes and messages of the text.

Sometimes they are a way of looking at the themes of the text in a setting different than the biblical one— one more familiar to audiences today. In some cases, you could think of them as a choir anthem, building off the biblical text.

Using this book

This volume is one of two. The dramas in this book are related to the themes of worship for festivals and for Sundays from Advent to Pentecost. The second volume includes dramas for Sundays in the season of Pentecost. The Revised Common Lectionary, in use by many denominations, is the lectionary around which these volumes are organized.

The dramas are listed in the table of contents according the festival or Sunday of the church year to which each drama best belongs. However, there are indexes in the back of the book that organize by Bible text and by key idea. Of course, you can use these dramas wherever they fit best for you and your setting.

Each drama includes a list of characters and suggests a setting and props needed. Each drama is followed by the Prayer of the Day: This prayer generally sets the tone of the day, capturing the themes of the readings. It is included to assist worship planners as they try to create a cohesive, meaningful worship event. Please do not feel bound to use the Prayer of the Day that is listed. There are sources for new prayers (such as *Sundays*

and Seasons, published annually by Augsburg Fortress)
that may use language that feels less "churchy."

Beginning comments for the new director

None of these dramas is very complicated to stage,
but here are some things for you to remember:

• The worship service should be about the Word and
  Sacraments, not about the drama. Because of this, you
  will want to move into and out of the drama quickly,
  with a minimum of fuss. Practice, if you have props
  or a setting that needs to be set before and struck
  after. Move the stuff in and out quickly, quietly, and
  with intention.

• The people you ask to participate in the dramas
  should have clear voices, expressive faces, and a com-
  fortable public manner. They will need to practice
  these dramas ahead of time so they can concentrate
  on what their characters are saying and doing rather
  than on what comes next and where they are supposed to be standing. They don't have to memorize
  their lines, but they need to know them well enough
  to be able to make eye contact with each other and
  the audience when needed.

• Feel free to cast the characters across gender and age
  lines when appropriate. In most cases, a woman can
  play a man's part or visa versa with a couple of slight

changes in the lines of those who refer to him or her.
You might even experiment with casting a child or
a woman as God's voice, to help people stretch and
keep things less predictable. When names are used
in the dramas, use names that reflect the breadth of
ethnicities in your community.

- Keep it simple. Because you will be in a space that is
  used for other purposes, it may have steps and other
  hazards for the actors, and because the dramas are
  short, simple is the best. Keep costuming, set, and
  stage movement to a minimum.

- Try to arrange for good lighting. Most church sanctu-
  aries were not built for excellent illumination for the
  area where you will most likely be performing. If pos-
  sible, try to buy or rent a few stage lights. Hang them
  45 degrees to the actors. That angle creates the fewest
  strange shadows of faces, which makes it easier to
  understand what they actors are saying (because you
  can see their faces better).

- If you can also have the ability to dim the lights, that
  would add enormously to your ability to set a mood.
  A spotlight can be okay, but it would be more helpful
  to invest in better general lighting that you can
  control and adjust.

- Use your PA system if it is any good at all. If you have
  wireless microphones for the actors, that is the best,
  but there may not be enough of them to go around.

If your system is not very flexible, you may want to rely on a reader's theater style of staging rather than asking actors to pass microphones around. Set the actors up with music stands arranged around a few standing microphones. Identify someone to explain the setting at the beginning. Some of the dramas lend themselves to this nicely. With some, this style won't be as interesting, but it will be much better than having the primary energy of the drama be about getting the microphone to the person who is going to speak next!

Just like anything we do in worship, the point is to glorify God and to help people come to new under-standings about their relationship with God. The dramas are a cog in the worship wheel, no more important than other parts of the worship service. For a while, dramas will seem special (and some people may even see them as offensive or not worshipful). But if you do them enough, worshipers will come to see them as just another way of exploring what God is doing with us in this worship service.

The Unveiling

Text: Matthew 9:12-13

Key idea: We hide behind masks of goodness, especially in church.

Characters: Bob
                   John
                   (They both wear masks over their faces.)

Setting: a church sanctuary

Props: trash receptacle, chair

Bob: Hey, hey, hey, hi!

John: Hi, hi, hi!

Bob: How's it going?

John: Great! Great! How's the wife and kids?

Bob: Great! Great! *(Drops his head)* Not so great!

John: Not so great?

Bob: *(takes his mask off)* I can't do it anymore. I'm sorry. If you really want to know, my marriage is falling apart.

John: Wow! Wow! Wow! You'd better get out of here before someone finds out!

Bob: Why?

John: This is a church! We can't keep people like you in here! *(Standing on chair)* Usher! Usher! There's a sinner here! He'll mess up the whole thing!

Bob: But, I can't help it. I have problems. I have these sins in my life, and I . . .

John: *(covering ears and singing so he can't hear)* I can't listen to this! La, la, la, la, la . . .

Bob: Stop it! Stop it! If I can't be open here, where else can I go?

John: La, la, la, la . . .

Bob: Just take it off your mask for a second. Just try it!

John: What mask?

Bob: The mask on your head!

John: There's no . . . *(Feels his head)* Oh, so there is!

Bob: Take it off for a second.

John: Is anyone looking?

Bob: No.

John: *(takes off mask)* Hey, it's a lot easier to breathe now. Did it mess up my hair?

Bob: A little. You can put the mask back on if you want to.

John: Why would I want to do that?

Bob: Well, I think it'd be easier for you to ignore me that way.

John: Hey, to be honest, life's no picnic at my house either.

Bob: Really?

John: Yeah.

Bob: Do you still think I should leave the church?

John: No. Sorry about that. I guess that mask was cutting off oxygen to my brain. I'll tell you what. Why don't we go out for lunch. You could probably use a listening ear.

Bob: Yeah, I could. What should we do with these masks?

John: *(Drops his mask into the trash.)* Let 'em go out with the rest of the trash.

Bob: Okay. *(Drops his mask into the trash as he and John exit.)*

O God, the strength of those who hope in you:
Be present and hear our prayers; and, because in the
weakness of our mortal nature we can do nothing
good without you, give us the help of your grace,
so that in keeping your commandments we may
please you in will and deed; through your Son,
Jesus Christ our Lord. Amen

Insomnia

Text: Matthew 11:16-19, 25-30

Key idea: Shame distracts us from God's love.

Character: Jason

(This drama is a monologue.)

Setting: Jason lies in bed with a cool light pointing down on him. Eerie music underscores an offstage voice speaking his thoughts.

Props: bed, nightstand, alarm clock

Jason: I got the charts. Got the stats. Laptop's in my office. Judy! Judy thinks the meeting's at 10 o'clock, but it's really at 10:30. Call her in the morning. Can't forget to call her in the morning. I should write that down. No, don't write it down. It's 4:40 in the morning. Go to sleep. Go to sleep. Go to sleep. Relax. Relax. Come on. Come on. Come on. It's 4:40! I have to get up in an hour. God, I'm begging you. Make me sleep. I can't go to that meeting tomorrow on two hours of sleep. Breathe. Breathe.

I'm not spending enough time with the kids. I'm a workaholic. I'm an office junky. I never let the kids

keep me awake like this. I'm scarring them. I have to
find time to spend with the kids. What's important to
you, Jason, work or the kids? What kind of example
are you setting? I should schedule a date with them.
Mental note: schedule date with the kids. I should
write that down or I'll forget. Get up and write it
down. They deserve it . . . But it's 4:43 in the morning! No one writes notes to themselves in the middle
of the night. Only crazy people do that.

I'm going crazy. I think I'm going crazy. Just breathe.
Just breathe. This is all a bad dream. God, please
wake me up from this bad dream. Wait. If I'm asleep,
don't wake me up. . . . But I'm not asleep. Who am I
kidding? I'm a crazy insomniac, a failure of a parent
whose kids are being scarred because their dad
doesn't spend enough time with them, because he's
always at work, and he's going to lose his job because
he's not prepared for the meeting tomorrow, then I
won't be able to pay the mortgage and we'll all end
up on the street, living in our minivan, and I won't
be able to pay the VISA bill . . . Oh, the VISA bill!
I forgot to pay the VISA bill. And the library books
are late, too. They're going to send the library cops
after me. How's it going to look to be dragged away
in handcuffs by the library police? There is no such
thing as library cops. What am I thinking?

Go to sleep. Go to sleep. Go to sleep. Relax. Relax.
Come on. Come on. Come on. It's 4:50. I have to get
up in an hour! God, I'm begging you. Make me sleep.
Make me sleep. Knock me out. I can't live like this
anymore. I'm panting. Just breathe. Just relax. I can't
relax. I have to get the kids up for day care. No, wait.
They don't go to day care. They go to school. What
am I thinking? Oh, God, lock me up and save me
from myself. I just need some time away. I just need
a day to sit by the pool and go to sleep. I need sleep.
That's what I need! Oh, God, please make me sleep.
I can't face tomorrow like this. Please, God. Please,
God, please . . .

*God of glory and love, peace comes from you
alone. Send us as peacemakers and witnesses to
your kingdom, and fill our hearts with joy in your
promises of salvation; through your Son,
Jesus Christ our Lord. Amen*

The Diner

Text: Luke 10:38-42

Key idea: The work of our hands is the work of the
Spirit.

Characters: Mary
Marilyn
Bobby
Leslie
Tom
Greg
Arthur
God *(offstage voice)*

Set: a diner

Props: 3 restaurant tables, 6 water glasses, 6 coffee cups,
2 plates of sandwiches, Chinese checkers *(or another
board game)*, laptop computer, coffee pot, menus

*Marilyn and Bobby sit down-right in quiet but heated
discussion over a marital issue.*

*Leslie, Tom, and Greg sit down-left playing Chinese
checkers (or another board game).*

Mary enters stage left carrying a pot of coffee to Leslie, Tom, and Greg. As she's pouring, Arthur enters stage right in a coat and tie, carrying a laptop computer.

Mary grabs a menu from up-stage and shows Arthur to his table center-stage.

Mary exits stage left and returns with two plates of sand-wiches for Marilyn and Bobby. As she sets them down, Tom holds his coffee cup in the air, motioning to Mary that he needs a refill.

As Mary begins to cross to Tom's table, Bobby calls to get her attention . . .

Bobby: Waitress! Waitress!

(Mary turns around and hurries back to Bobby.)

Bobby: You brought me the wrong sandwich.

Mary: You don't want egg salad?

Bobby: No. I said *turkey* with *potato salad* on the side.

Mary: I'm sorry. I'll go have Ed make you a turkey.

Marilyn: He's already a turkey, honey. He doesn't need a cook to help him.

Bobby: Now, what's that supposed to mean?

Marilyn: Make of it what you will, Bobby.

(Tom puts his coffee cup in the air again. Mary notices it.)

Bobby: You know, you don't have to share your disgust with the whole world.

(Bobby quietly continues his response while Mary, trying to avoid being witness to their marital discord, crosses to Tom's table.)

Mary: More coffee?

Tom: Yeah. *(Begins to exit)* Hey, could we split a plate of fries?

Mary: Sure. *(Mary begins to exit again.)*

Leslie: And could I get some "chai"?

Mary: Some what?

Leslie: "Chai." On ice.

Mary: *(frustrated)* I have no idea what you are talking about.

Leslie: It's a tea. I think it's from India.

Greg: No, I think it's from Tibet or something.

Tom: No, it's a Taiwan thing.

Leslie: No, it's from India.

Mary: I think it's from New Jersey!

Leslie: New Jersey? Forget it. We want international tea. Just get the fries.

Mary: *(sarcastically)* My pleasure.

(Mary exits stage-left and returns with coffee for Leslie, Tom, and Greg. She then crosses to Arthur who's staring at his laptop.)

Mary: What can I get for you? *(Arthur pays no attention to her.)* Excuse me. Sir . . . Sir, have you decided what you want?

Arthur: Yes.

Mary: *(pause)* Would you mind telling me what that might be?

Arthur: What time do you get off work?

Mary: Excuse me?

Arthur: What time do you get off work?

Mary: Sir, I'm all alone here today because Janet called in sick! Now, I'd love to play along with your little come on, but I don't have the time. Now, what do you want?

Arthur: Trust me, I'm not coming on to you.
I just want . . .

Bobby: Waitress!

Mary: What?

Bobby: Is my sandwich ready?

Arthur: I just . . .

Mary: *(to Bobby)* Just give me a second!
(To Arthur) Sir, what did you say?

Arthur: I just want someone to . . .

Greg: Waitress!

God: Mary.

Mary: What?

Greg: Does the word *fries* mean anything to you?

Mary: *(to Greg)* Just give me a second! *(To Arthur)* Sir,
I don't have all day! What do you want?

Arthur: It's asking way too much.

Marilyn: Waitress!

God: Mary.

Mary: *(to Marilyn)* Hold tight!

Leslie, Tom, Greg: *(chanting)* Fries. Fries. Fries . . .

Arthur: I'm sorry, I . . .

Bobby: Waitress!

Leslie, Tom, Greg: *(chanting)* Fries. Fries. Fries . . .

God: Mary!

Mary: *(to Leslie, Tom, Greg)* Please!

Marilyn: Waitress!

Mary: *(to Marilyn)* Please!

Arthur: I just want someone to talk to!

Mary: *(reaching her boiling point)* You want someone to
talk to? YOU WANT SOMEONE TO TALK TO?

God: *(offstage voice)* Mary, stop!

(Everyone except Mary freezes.)

Mary: What? What do you want? Janet called in sick. I don't have the time . . .

God: Mary, imagine the possibilities here.

Mary: What are you talking about?

God: *I'm* working here, too . . . in the lives of these people. Look deeper. What do you see?

(Mary crosses to Marilyn and Bobby, who are caught in confrontational gestures.)

Mary: Well, every time these two come in they're fighting.

God: Yes, their marriage is falling apart.

Mary: *(walking to Leslie, Tom, and Greg)* I don't know what it is with these three. All they do is come in and play board games and drink coffee.

God: Why?

Mary: I guess they don't have anywhere else to go.

God: Right. They're looking for a home. What about Arthur over there?

Mary: *(walking to Arthur)* Well, he's easy. He just wants someone to talk to.

God: Imagine what would happen if every day you took just a couple moments to listen, to show you care.

Mary: But I . . .

God: Just imagine it.

* * *

O God, you see how busy we are with many things. Turn us to listen to your teachings and lead us to choose the one things which will not be taken from us, Jesus Christ our Lord. Amen

Voices

Text: Romans 8:26-39

Key idea: Christ comes to liberate us from our past.

Characters: Daughter *(an adult)*
Father *(offstage voice)*
Mother *(offstage voice)*
Jesus *(offstage voice)*

Setting: an office

Props: desk, chair, computer, and other office equipment

(The Daughter is working at her desk.)

Father: *(offstage voice)* Look at you. I told you that was a dead-end job. Who are you kidding?

Daughter: *(to the air)* You're not real.

Mother: *(offstage voice)* Honey, I'm not saying we're always right, but you have to admit you have a tendency to act before you think.

Daughter: *(standing)* Stop it.

Mother: I'm not trying to make you feel bad. I just know you and the way you think.

Daughter: You don't know me.

Father: I know you. You're a selfish little girl. You never pay any attention to anyone but yourself.

Daughter: Stop it.

Father: The truth hurts, doesn't it?

Mother: You know we never had this sort of trouble with your sister.

Daughter: What am I doing that's so wrong?

Mother: It's not what you're doing. It's what you're not doing.

Daughter: What am I "not doing"?

Father: How blind can you be?

Daughter: I'm not going to listen to you! You're not even real.

Father: You're just selfish!

Mother: Belligerent!

Jesus: *(offstage voice)* Brilliant!

Father: Irresponsible!

Mother: Inconsiderate!

Jesus: Incredible!

Father: You're a disgrace!

Mother: You're an embarrassment!

Jesus: You are fearfully and wonderfully made. You are precious in my sight. I knit you together in your mother's womb and I have watched you every moment of your life. I know the number of hairs on your head. I know your hopes and your dreams. I was there at the mountaintops and I am here in the valley. And those other voices will come and go, but I will never leave. I loved you yesterday. I love you today. And I will love you tomorrow. Nothing, my precious child, nothing will ever separate you from my love.

Daughter: Excuse me, sir. I know the other voices but not yours. What's your name?

Jesus: Oh, I've been called many things . . . but my name is Jesus.

O God, your ears are open always to the prayers of your servants. Open our hearts and minds to you, that we may live in harmony with your will and receive the gifts of your Spirit; through your Son, Jesus Christ our Lord. Amen

I Think I'm Lost

Text: Colossians 2:6-15

Key idea: We can't make it on our own.

Characters: Mindy
                   God *(offstage voice)*

Setting: unspecified

Props: three books

(Mindy wanders around stage with three books. She references one and goes one way. Then looks at another and goes a different way.)

God: *(offstage voice)* Excuse me, may I help you?

Mindy: No, I'm fine. Let's see, this map says that success lies down this road. But this map says success is that way. What's this one say? Success is . . . go down this road take a left. Now I'm really confused.

God: Is there anything I can do?

Mindy: No, no, I have it all under control. *Eeny, meenie, miny, moe. Catch a tiger by the toe. If he hollers, let him go. Eeny, meenie, miny, moe.* Okay, so that road's out. My mother said to pick the very best one and you are not it. Okay, I guess I'll go that way.

God: Trust me! Don't go that way!

Mindy: Excuse me?

God: You won't find what you're looking for that way.

Mindy: How do you know?

God: I'm God.

Mindy: I see. Then I guess it's that way, right?

God: No! Don't go that way either.

Mindy: Well, one of these maps has to be right.

God: Which maps do you have?

Mindy: These are the most popular books on success on the market.

God: Why are you trusting those road maps?

Mindy: Well, everyone else is.

God: What if all of those writers change their mind and decide that success is down some other road. Will you buy their new book?

Mindy: If everyone else does.

God: If everyone else jumped off a cliff, would you?

Mindy: You sound like my mother.

God: Actually your mother sounds like me.

Mindy: Huh?

God: Forget it. Listen, if you want to find out what success is really all about, you need to chuck those road maps and get a hold of a new one.

Mindy: What's the name of it?

God: I'll spell it for you

(Mindy grabs a pad of paper.)

God: B-I-B-L-E.

Mindy: Who wrote it?

God: Me.

Mindy: Me who?

God: Me—me!

Mindy: Never heard of him.

God: Me—God!

Mindy: Oh, I get it.

God: No, you don't. If you did, you wouldn't be spending your time on those other maps.

Mindy: So, you'll show me how to find success? prestige? wealth?

God: I'll show you how to find success, but please understand that success has nothing to do with prestige or wealth.

Mindy: Okay fine, whatever. Just give me the directions, and I'll leave and get out of your hair.

God: No, no, no, you can't go there by yourself. I have to take you there.

Mindy: Well, that's awfully nice of you, but I like to travel alone.

God: Then you'll never find what you're looking for.

Mindy: I'll tell you what. I'll get one of your Bibles and get the directions out of there, and I'll find success in no time. You just watch.

God: You won't understand the directions without my help.

Mindy: Hey, I was a Girl Scout. I can do it by myself. Trust me.

God: No, trust me.

Mindy: Don't worry. If I get lost, I'll give you a buzz.

God: If that's the way you want it.

Mindy: Let's see, which way would I go to find a Bible?

God: Well, you could . . .

Mindy: That's okay! That's okay! I'll find it myself.

O God, your ears are open always
to the prayer of your servants. Open our hearts and
minds to you, that we may live in harmony with your
will and receive the gifts of your Spirit; through your
Son, Jesus Christ our Lord. Amen

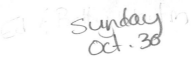

Checkbook Theology

Text: Luke 12:13-21

Key idea: How do we distinguish needs from wants? How do we put God first?

Characters: Ken
                   God *(offstage voice)*

Setting: a study or den in Ken's home, where Ken sits balancing his checkbook

Props: desk, chair, pen, receipts, checkbook

Ken: Oh, please balance. Please, dear God, make my checkbook balance. Abracadabra. Please, please, please balance.

God: Excuse me, Ken, that's not the way I work.

Ken: Oh, God, I'm glad you're here. I got a note from the bank and it sounds like they're really mad. I wrote some checks that were kind of rubbery, kind of bouncy . . .

God: Yes, I know.

Ken: So, I now take my checkbook and lay it at your feet and say, "Please, please, please fix it, Almighty Fixer."

God: Ken, let's get real for a second. It's time you took some responsibility for your spending.

Ken: I'm responsible for my spending. I spend every cent I have—and more.

God: I know, but you're not spending responsibly.

Ken: No, that's where you're wrong. The problem is I just don't have enough to spend.

God: Excuse me, I'm not wrong . . . never have been and never will be. Now open your checkbook and tell me why you wrote the check on March 1st.

Ken: March 1st. . . March 1st. . . Here it is. Oh, well, I . . . uh . . . was at the mall and I was really depressed because of . . . uh . . . all the hatred in the world, that's it, so I bought some in-line skates. And they made me feel happy again.

God: Okay, now explain to me the relationship between in-line skates and hatred.

Ken: Well, with the skates I became happier because they made me think of summer when I could use them. And as you know, crime goes up in the summer . . . so . . . I can use them to quickly fight crime on the streets where I live.

God: Ken, what color is the sky in your world?

Ken: Okay, okay, okay, you're right. Dumb purchase.

God: Tell me about the purchase on March 5th.

Ken: Well, that seems to be a check to a music store. Let's see, I bought some CDs.

God: Some CDs?

Ken: A few CDs.

God: A few?

Ken: All right, six CDs.

God: There we go.

Ken: I needed those CDs.

God: Why?

Ken: Because they were on sale. If I didn't act quickly, they might have gone back up to the regular price.

God: But why did you *need* them?

Ken: Because . . . you're right. I didn't need them.

God: All right now we're getting somewhere. Now, Ken, tell me about the check you wrote to me this past month.

Ken: What are you talking about?

God: I mean the check you wrote to help see my work done in the world.

Ken: I'm not sure I understand.

God: Your offering. The check you wrote to church.

Ken: Oh, I see what you mean. *(Looks through the checkbook.)* Um, apparently I didn't write one for that specific purpose recently.

God: Recently?

Ken: Lately.

God: Lately?

Ken: In quite some time.

God: Bingo.

Ken: Sorry.

God: Ken, let's look at next month. The past is over. Let's plan for next month. What are you going to do with my money next month?

Ken: Your money?

God: Yes, my money.

Ken: Well, I don't know what you're going to do with your money, but I'm going to take mine and . . .

God: Ken, excuse me, but that money you get is *my* gift to you, and I want you to spend it wisely. Now, what's your plan?

Ken: I need a plan?

God: Yes.

Ken: But I don't know where to start.

God: Start with me. Always start with me.

---

*Almighty God, judge of us all, you have placed
in our hands the wealth we call our own. Give us such
wisdom by your Spirit that our possessions may not
be a cures in our lives, but instruments for blessing;
through your Son, Jesus Christ our Lord. Amen*

Perspectives

Text: Ephesians 4:25—5:2

Key idea: Closing ourselves to one another leaves us lonely.

Characters: Husband
                     Wife
                     Child *(12-15 years old)*

Setting: unspecified

Props: none

(The Husband stands stage right, the Wife stands stage left, and the Child stands center stage.)

Husband: *(to the audience)* Do I love her? Hmmm . . . Well, that's the million-dollar-question isn't it?

Wife: *(to the audience)* I need affection. I want to know that he's proud of me and that he respects me. But when I look in his eyes I see anger and judgment.

Child: *(to the audience)* Something's happening. I hear it in their voices while I'm lying in bed. I can tell. Something's happening.

Husband: I don't know what she wants from me. I'm not perfect. I know that, but I'm doing the best I can. She says I don't talk to her. Well, every time I try to tell her what's really on my mind, she ends up crying. So what am I supposed to do? I'll tell you what I do. I don't talk, because she couldn't take it if I did.

Wife: I loved him so much. He was everything to me. I always thought he was so intelligent, and he is. I love his mind. He doesn't love mine, though. He thinks I'm stupid. He won't admit it, but you can tell in the way he talks about me to other people. When he tells a story about me to his friends, they all shake their heads and laugh.

Child: I hate being at home when they're both there. You could slice the tension in the air with a knife. They don't talk to each other. They just exchange necessary information. I can tell my dad's checked out. He's gone more, and when he is home, all he does is nap and watch TV. And my mom just cleans and cleans and cleans. I guess that's the one thing she thinks she can still control.

Husband: I hate bedtime the most. The silence is like this big, wool blanket suffocating us. The whole thing's become a bad dream.

Wife: I've taken to sleeping on the couch and falling asleep with the TV on. I just can't take his silence. The other night our child came out and asked me if I was okay. I'd been crying. I said I'd just watched a sad movie on TV. He knew I was lying.

Child: They both are unhappy. I can hear it in their voices. I should have done something sooner. I knew this was coming. I saw the same thing happen in my friend's house. And now he's splitting time between two houses. I can't do that. Why should I have to do that? I'm never getting married.

Husband: I want to fix this.

Wife: I want out.

Child: I want a home.

Almighty and everlasting God, you are always more ready to hear than we are to pray, and to give more than we either desire or deserve. Pour upon us the abundance of your mercy, forgiving us those things of which our conscience is afraid, and giving us those good things for which we are not worthy to ask, except through the merit of your Son, Jesus Christ our Lord. Amen

I'm Parched

Text: Luke 12:32-40

Key idea: Treasures on earth won't last.

Characters: Drew
  God *(offstage voice)*

Setting: Unspecified, but a glass of water sits on a stand, stage left.

Props: a cell phone, newspaper, laptop computer, portable TV, and trophy

(Drew enters, obviously tired and thirsty, and carrying all six props listed above.)

Drew: Parched! Parched! Parched! God Almighty, have mercy on me. I'm parched!

God: *(offstage voice)* What is it that you'd like?

Drew: Something to quench my thirst.

God: Look to your left. *(To Drew's left is a glass of water on a pedestal.)* Go take a drink.

Drew: Oh, thank you, Lord. Thank you!

(Drew rises and walks toward the glass of water. Drew stands staring at the glass)

God: What's wrong?

Drew: I don't know how to drink it.

God: Just pick it up and drink it.

Drew: I can't. I don't have enough hands.

God: Well, put those things down.

Drew: I can't. I need these things.

God: You *need* them?

Drew: Yeah, they're my special treasures. This phone keeps me connected with my broker. The computer let's me take work home. The TV is . . . the TV is like a little slice of heaven. I get 63 channels.

God: The "slice of heaven" thing kind of offends me. If you don't put those things down, you'll never be able to drink the water.

Drew: *(stops to think)* Could I have a straw?

God: Sorry.

Drew: You're mean.

God: No, I'm not. I just know what's best for you. Let go of that stuff.

Drew: Supposing I do, what'll I get in return?

God: Your thirst will be quenched.

Drew: Well, these things do that.

God: Then why are you still thirsty?

Drew: Well, they just quench it for a little while and then I have to find something else.

God: If you drink from my well, you will thirst no longer. Trust me. Let go.

Drew: Easy for you to say, you don't get cable.

God: Just taste it!

Drew: I want to trust you. Really I do. But I think I'd like to try a couple other things first.

God: Like what?

Drew: I think I'll go and throw a little more energy into my career. A new car might really do the trick. Maybe I'll try some drugs or maybe I'll try to get in shape. Who knows? If those things don't work, maybe I'll come back.

God: Quit chasing after the wind!

Drew: I'm not chasing the wind. I'm chasing a fine luxury automobile.

God: I'm not going to stop you.

Drew: As well you shouldn't. It's my life and I . . .

God: Can screw it up all by yourself. I'll be here, though. I'll be around for you when you are ready.

Drew: Right! Bye, now. *(While exiting)* Boy, I hate this cotton-mouth feeling.

Almighty and everlasting God, you are always more ready to hear than we are to pray, and to give more than we either desire or deserve. Pour upon us the abundance of your mercy, forgiving us those things of which our conscience is afraid, and giving us those good things for which we are not worthy to ask, except through the merit of your Son, Jesus Christ our Lord. Amen

My Plans

Text: Romans 12:1-8

Key idea: Trust God with our life plans.

Characters: Mario
                    God *(offstage voice)*

Setting: unspecified

Props: loose sheets of papers

Mario: *(running out on stage)* God, wait till you see what I've come up with. I've been doing some thinking about my life, and I think I'm really on to something. Here, I typed it all out for you. *(Removes some papers from his pocket.)* And trust me, you're going to want to bless this.

God: *(offstage voice)* Really?

Mario: Really. First things first: I got a call from a business recruiter who got my name from a buddy who works there, and the guy basically offered me a job, with a 10,000-dollar increase in pay. He said I could write my own job description. The catch is that it's in Seattle, but that's where Karen and I have been thinking about moving. So, Karen's talking to a friend of hers who runs a graphic-design firm there, and her friend . . .

God: Do you trust me?

Mario: Yes. Now, her friend says she could get Karen a job there in a minute. So we called the realtor and they said they could have the house sold in two weeks at the most. The kids are young enough . . .

God: Do you trust me?

Mario: *(butting in)* Yes. Now, the kids are young enough so they won't sweat a big move like this. I'm sure they'll even grow from it. Well, that's the plan. Take a look at it. Put your John Hancock on it *(lays plan on the ground)*, and meet me in Seattle. *(Begins to exit.)*

God: Don't go to Seattle.

Mario: What are you talking about? Weren't you listening? A 10,000-dollar pay increase! Karen's on board. Why aren't you?

God: Why don't you trust me?

Mario: I trust you. I just think in this case, you're *(whispering)* probably not right.

God: What was that?

Mario: *(whispering)* I said you're probably not . . . *(speaking normally)* Okay, I know you're perfect, but this opportunity is perfect. How can you not . . .

God: How can you not trust me? Have I ever failed you? Have you ever found that what I've done is wrong for you?

Mario: Well, what do *you* want me to do?

God: Stay where you are.

Mario: And stagnate.

God: I am doing something amazing right around you. I want you to be a part of it.

Mario: What? What are you doing?

God: I'll reveal it to you at the right time. In the meantime, just wait.

Mario: Why won't you tell me?

God: Because I want you to trust me.

Mario: I need a new challenge, though.

God: Trust me.

Mario: What could possibly be wrong with moving?

God: Trust me.

Mario: What am I going to tell Karen?

God: TRUST me.

Mario: Okay.

God of all creation, you reach out to call people of all nations to your kingdom. As you gather disciples from near and far, count us also among those who boldly confess your Son, Jesus Christ as Lord. Amen

Take My Life

Text: Luke 13:10-17

Key idea: Freeing ourselves for service.

Characters: Ingrid
Jesus *(offstage voice)*

Setting: a church service

Props: A daily planner and a beeper. A hymnal would be appropriate if the church uses hymnals instead of overhead projections.

(Ingrid stands and sings the last verse of the hymn "Take My Life, that I May Be," Lutheran Book of Worship *406, text by Frances R. Havergal, tune by William H. Havergal.)*

Ingrid: I am trusting you, Lord Jesus; Never let me fall. I am trusting you forever, and for all. *(praying)* I just want to serve you, Jesus.

Jesus: *(offstage voice)* I want you to serve me, Ingrid.

Ingrid: I want to be on your team.

Jesus: I want you to be on my team.

Ingrid: I'm ready.

Jesus: No, you're not.

Ingrid: Yes, I am, Jesus.

Jesus: No, you're not, Ingrid.

Ingrid: What's the problem?

Jesus: Ingrid, you're carrying so much around. When do you have time to serve on my team?

(Ingrid's beeper goes off.)

Ingrid: Hold on. *(Checks her beeper.)*

Jesus: Ingrid . . . ?

Ingrid: Just wait one second. I'd better write this number down. *(Opens her daily planner and writes down a message.)*

Jesus: While you have that open, tell me where I fit on your schedule.

Ingrid: Let's see. I think I can fit you in on Sunday mornings.

Jesus: You think you can fit me in?

Ingrid: It's going to be tight. Jamie's got skating, and it is football season.

Jesus: How about Wednesday nights? Can you make it to the midweek service?

Ingrid: Can't. There's a great line-up on TV tonight.

Jesus: Perhaps you could help with that free-oil change your church is doing. You're pretty good with cars.

Ingrid: *(Checking her schedule)* I'd like to, but Jack's got soccer practice that morning, and I always mow the lawn on Saturdays.

Jesus: Ingrid, let me get this straight. You want to be on my team, but you don't want to do anything?

Ingrid: No, you're misunderstanding me . . .

Jesus: No, you're misunderstanding *me. (Speaking slowly so Ingrid understands every word.)* I'm doing something with my team, the church, and I want you to be a part of it.

Ingrid: What are you doing?

Jesus: Look at the world around you. What kind of shape is it in?

Ingrid: It's a mess.

Jesus: Right. I put the church on earth to deal with the mess.

Ingrid: Well, Jesus, I'll give you an "E" for effort, but I don't think the church is equipped to . . .

Jesus: No, that's where you're wrong! When churches listen to my voice, and follow where I lead . . . there's nothing on earth more powerful. *Nothing.*

Ingrid: What? Do you want us to overthrow the government?

Jesus: No, I want you to be a part of a conspiracy of love. I want you to love me and everyone around you with your whole life, your whole being. When people see you, I want them to see me. Not enough people know that I love them. I am a parent. I am crazy about my children. I am passionate about them, Ingrid. I need you to help carry this message.

Ingrid: That's a pretty tall order.

Jesus: Ingrid, I didn't put the church on earth to give people a reason to go out for Sunday brunch. *(Pause)* Now, I will accomplish my purposes with you or without you. Are you with me, or will I encroach too much on your schedule?

Ingrid: You're serious.

Jesus: Serious enough to give my life for this cause. Now, what are you willing to give?

God of all creation, you reach out to call people of all nations to your kingdom. As you gather disciples from near and far, count us also among those who boldly confess your Son, Jesus Christ as Lord. Amen

I Have Needs

Text: Mark 8:27-38

Key idea: Selfishness versus servanthood.

Characters: Psychologist
Mr. Johnson

Setting: a psychologist's office

Props: two chairs, a clipboard for the psychologist

Psychologist: Well, Mr. Johnson, why are you here this morning?

Johnson: Well, Doctor, I've been pretty down lately, and I don't know what to do.

Psychologist: How are things at home?

Johnson: Oh, not so good. I feel like my family takes advantage of me.

Psychologist: Really? What's led you to that conclusion?

Johnson: No one does anything nice for me. My kids think I'm there to serve their every need. It's always, "Get me some juice! I want dinner! Put in a movie!" I'm a person. I'm not their slave.

Psychologist: How old are your kids?

Johnson: Two and four.

Psychologist: Mr. Johnson, when kids are that young they need a parent to pour their drinks, and get their food.

Johnson: See, you've bought into it too! How are they ever going to learn to respect me if they don't think about my needs! Why don't they ever get my juice? Why don't they ever make me dinner.

Psychologist: They're very young, Mr. Johnson.

Johnson: Nah, that's just a trick they use to get out of responsibility.

Psychologist: Let's talk about your wife. How's your marriage?

Johnson: Miserable. My wife doesn't care about me.

Psychologist: Why do you say that?

Johnson: She never does anything nice for me! She doesn't give me backrubs or anything!

Psychologist: Does your wife work?

Johnson: Nah, she just watches the kids.

Psychologist: That's work.

Johnson: Yeah, right.

Psychologist: Do you ever watch the kids?

Johnson: I would if they ever did anything nice for me.

Psychologist: Mr. Johnson, how do you display affection toward your wife?

Johnson: What do you mean?

Psychologist: What do you do to let her know you love her?

Johnson: You're trying to trick me into doing something nice for her, and I'm not going to do it. I'll do something nice for her as soon as she does something nice for me.

Psychologist: Mr. Johnson, can you spell pig?

Johnson: P-I-G. What's that got to do with my problem?

Psychologist: Nothing. It just made me feel good to have you spell pig. Let's move on. How's work?

Johnson: Terrible. They don't appreciate me there.

Psychologist: What makes you say that?

Johnson: I've been working there for five years. First two months it was great, but ever since then, no one talks to me.

Psychologist: Why not?

Johnson: Oh, at some staff meeting several years ago, I suggested that everyone should chip in and buy me doughnuts.

Psychologist: Like . . . once a month?

Johnson: No, like once a day.

Psychologist: Doesn't that seem outlandish to you?

Johnson: I know. I can't believe they didn't go for it.

Psychologist: Mr. Johnson, do you know anything about Jesus Christ?

Johnson: *(sarcastically)* Yes, I know who Jesus Christ is.

Psychologist: Would you classify Jesus as a joyful person?

Johnson: I don't know. I guess.

Psychologist: You know if you look at the life of Jesus, his whole life was about serving others.

Johnson: And look where it got him!

Psychologist: Mr. Johnson, our time is up, but I think we should get together again next week.

Johnson: All right. Why don't you meet me at my office.

Psychologist: I don't do house calls.

Johnson: Not my house. My office.

Psychologist: I don't do office calls.

Johnson: Wow, touchy!

Psychologist: See you next week.

Johnson: Bye.

O God, you declare your almighty power chiefly in showing mercy and pity. Grant us the fullness of your grace, that, pursuing what you have promised, we may share your heavenly glory; through your Son, Jesus Christ our Lord. Amen

The Gift

Text: Luke 15:1-10 (v. 8)

Key idea: The generosity of God.

Characters: Man
                      Narrator *(offstage voice)*
                      Boy

Setting: a park, with the occasional sound of birds in the background, and occasional piano sound effects

Props: a picnic table

(The Man sits stage left on a picnic table. As the drama begins, the piano plays a repetitive, grumpy phrase.)

Narrator: *(offstage voice)* Once upon a time there lived a bitter, bitter man with little, little faith and a big, big attitude.

Man: I'm grumpy! I'm ornery! And I'm not going to take it anymore!

Narrator: So the bitter, bitter man sat in his bitter, bitter mind without ever recognizing the gifts the Giver had given him.

Man: The Giver? What Giver? I don't see any Giver. All I see is gloom and doom. Gloom and doom!

Narrator: But, sir, look around you! Your life is surrounded by the gifts of the Giver.

Man: Where? I don't see any gifts.

Narrator: Open your eyes!

Man: The sun's too bright.

Narrator: Smell the flowers.

Man: I've got allergies.

Narrator: This is the day the Giver has made!

Man: Send it back! I want a refund! *(Begins to pout.)*

Narrator: So the bitter, bitter man sat in his bitter, bitter mind, and the days went back and the days went forth *(Tempo slows on piano.)* like a heavy pendulum on a cheap . . . grandfather . . . clock. *(Piano stops.)* And he never went anywhere and he never loved anyone, and slowly but surely the bitter, bitter man became a bitter, bitter man. But then one day . . .

(Sound cue: Birds singing.)

Boy: *(approaching the bench)* Excuse me, sir.

Man: What?

Boy: I'm here.

Man: You're here?

Boy: I'm here.

Man: For *what* are you here?

Boy: For *you* I am here.

Man: Go away, lad. I'm a bitter, bitter man.

Boy: I know. May I sit with you?

Man: It's a free world.

(The Boy climbs up and sits next to the Man. There is a long pause as the Boy studies the Man's expression.)

Boy: You are sad.

Man: Yes, I am sad.

Boy: Why are you sad?

Man: The darkness is so heavy.

Boy: *(Reaches in his backpack and takes out a flashlight.)* Here.

Man: What's this?

Boy: It's a flashlight.

Man: I can see it's a flashlight!

Boy: Turn it on.

Man: *(Turns on the flashlight. The lights warm his skin.)* That's nice.

Boy: Are you thirsty?

Man: I'm parched.

Boy: *(Takes out a thermos.)* Here. Drink.

Man: *(Tales a drink.)* That's good.

Boy: It's living water.

Man: Yes, it is.

Boy: *(pause)* Are you sad still?

Man: Yes.

Boy: Why?

Man: The Giver hates me. I was cruel.

Boy: No, the Giver loves you. It was the Giver who sent the light. And it was the Giver who sent the water. And the Giver sent me, too, and when I grow up I will die the death so you don't have to.

Man: Oh, I couldn't ask that of you.

Boy: Oh, sir, I love you. I would have it no other way.

Man: *(pause)* What's your name, son?

Boy: My mama calls me Jesus, but you can call me friend. *(The Boy takes the Man's hand.)*

Man: Thank you, friend.

O God, you declare your almighty power chiefly in showing mercy and pity. Grant us the fullness of your grace, that, pursuing what you have promised, we may share your heavenly glory; through your Son, Jesus Christ our Lord. Amen

Is God In?

Text: Mark 10:2-16

Key idea: Jesus has time for us.

Note: This sketch highlights the misconception that many people have of God. It should be performed with a follow-up biblical message on God's true character.

Characters: Chuck *(a man born around 1965-1970)*
Secretary *(offstage voice)*
God *(offstage voice)*

Setting: a bare stage, with background music playing on cue

Props: none

Chuck: Excuse me. Hello! Anyone there?

Secretary: *(offstage voice)* Yeah, what do you want?

Chuck: I'd like to speak to God. Is he in?

Secretary: No, he's on vacation in the Bahamas. Of course he's in!

Chuck: May I speak to him?

Secretary: It depends. Have you been a good boy?

Chuck: Well . . .

Secretary: Let me check your file. Please hold.

(Music cue.)

Secretary: Oh, dear . . . Oh dear me . . . Well, I'll ask him if he wants to talk to you, but I'm not sure he's going to take the time. You were not a saint in high school. Please hold.

(Music cue.)

God: *(offstage voice)* Yeah, what do you want?

Chuck: Are you God?

God: No, I'm the tooth fairy. Of course it's me. What do you want?

Chuck: Well, I was just wondering . . .

God: Hold on. I got another call.

(Music cue.)

Okay, I'm back. Now, what's your name again?

Chuck: Chuck.

God: Charles?

Chuck: No, Chuck.

God: Are you the Charles who was convicted of armed robbery in July of 1952?

Chuck: It's Chuck, and I wasn't even born yet.

God: Are you the Charles who cheated on the S.A.T. in 1977?

Chuck: I was in grade school then. And it's Chuck!

God: Oh, yeah, Chuck, right. Are you the Chuck who was chased by the police on the golf course in 1987?

Chuck: That's me.

God: What do you want?

Chuck: Well, I was just wondering . . .

God: Please hold. I've got another call.

(Music cue)

Chuck: Boy, he's busy.

God: Okay, Sue, here's what I think you should do . . .

Chuck: I'm not Sue.

God: Who are you?

Chuck: I'm Chuck.

God: What do you want?

Chuck: I just . . .

God: Yes?

Chuck: I was just wondering . . .

God: Spit it out, boy.

Chuck: I was just wondering if . . .

God: I'm busy here! What do you want?

Chuck: I was just wondering if you like me.

God: Hmmm . . . What was your name again?

Chuck: Chuck! Oh, forget it.

Our Lord Jesus, you have endured the doubts and foolish questions of every generation. Forgive us for trying to be judge over you, and grant us the confident faith to acknowledge you as Lord. Amen

Christ Is Here to See You

Text: Matthew 22:1-14

Key idea: Life's frantic pace can exclude Jesus.

Characters: Jeff
                    Secretary

Setting: an office

Props: desk, phone, computer, papers, books, pens, and pencils

(Jeff dials the phone.)

Jeff: Hey, Bill. This is Jeff. Do you have a second? . . . Well, I'm kind of going through a crisis here. And I just need someone to bounce some ideas off of. . . . Well, I'm really struggling just getting through the day lately. I feel lost. I hate my job. Jan and I are barely getting along. The kids are . . . kids. I know this doesn't make sense but, I feel completely insignificant.

(Secretary enters with a message. She hands it to Jeff. He reads the message quickly.)

Jeff: *(referring to the message)* Hold on. Jesus Christ is here to see me? Not him again. This is not a good time. Ask him to come back later.

(Secretary exits.)

Jeff: Anyway . . . What's that? No, no, it isn't a midlife crisis. I think I just need a change. Collins offered me a pretty lucrative job offer. I'm thinking I might take it. What do you think?

(Secretary enters waving like she has another message.)

Jeff: What is it?

Secretary: He won't leave.

Jeff: Who won't leave?

Secretary: Jesus.

Jeff: Tell him I'm booked solid today. I just don't have the time.

Secretary: All right.

Jeff: You still there? Sorry. Jan thinks I need to get some religion. She keeps pushing me to go to church and to pray and stuff like that, but I just don't have the time. You know me, I'm not into that stuff.

(Secretary enters again.)

Jeff: What now?

Secretary: Mr. Christ, says he wants to help.

Jeff: I don't need his help! I can figure this out on my own.

Secretary: I think you should listen to him.

Jeff: I don't have time to listen to him. I've got a meeting in five minutes, and then I have to run home and take Janey to soccer practice. I've got to be back here at six o'clock tomorrow, and then I leave with Bob for that conference in Atlanta.

Secretary: Okay. *(Exits.)*

Jeff: Sorry for the interruption. Christ is out in my waiting room with a complete lack of understanding of my time and priorities. . . . Yeah, he's just waiting out there. . . . No, He doesn't have an appointment. He just popped in thinking I should drop everything for him. . . . I know! Who's he think he is? Well, listen, I have to go. I have a meeting. I trust you. . . . Yeah, take care. Bye.

(Secretary enters.)

Jeff: Did you get rid of him?

Secretary: Yes. He said he'd keep trying later. He wanted you to have this. *(Hands Jeff a Bible.)*

Jeff: A Bible? What am I supposed to do with this? I don't have time to read this. *(While exiting)* I have to run. If you need to get a hold of me, I'll have my cell phone on.

Secretary: Yes, sir.

(The Secretary exits.)

❈

*Almighty God, source of every blessing, your
generous goodness comes to us anew every day. By
the work of your Spirit lead us to acknowledge your
goodness, give thanks for your benefits, and serve
you in willing obedience; through your Son,
Jesus Christ our Lord. Amen*

Heavenly Hash

Text: Mark 10:17-31

Key idea: What is heaven and how do I get there?

Characters: Dr. Shaman Guru
                    Follower
                    Questioner
                    Announcer

Setting: a seminar suggested

Props: a podium and microphone, stool, flowers

Announcer: Ladies and gentlemen, please welcome the honorable Dr. Shaman Guru.

(Guru enters and sits center on a stool. The Follower approaches him and gives him some flowers.)

Guru: Thank you, child, the flower is you, and you are the flower. Therefore, take the flower and be you.

(Guru gives the flowers back to the Follower, who nods approvingly and sits back down.)

Guru: Thank you, children. Thank you for coming. I'm Dr. Shaman Guru. This is just the first of my visits to this part of the country. Today we are going to talk about *you*. About whatever's on your mind. The floor is as open as is the universe, so please, someone speak and I will answer.

Questioner: Dr. Guru, is there such a thing as heaven, and if so, how can I get there?

Guru: Ah, yes, heaven. *(Closes eyes as if in a trance.)* I'm in heaven right now. Okay, I'm back. *(Closes eyes.)* Wait, I'm in heaven again. *(Opens eyes.)* Okay, I'm back. Do you understand?

Questioner: No.

Guru: I see. I see *you.* I see heaven in you. Do you understand?

Questioner: Sorry.

Guru: Okay, yes, there is a heaven. It is the transcendental plain that all immortal children live on after they die. Anyone can go there for heaven is merely the hub of the immortal wheel. All religions are simply the spokes on the wheel leading to heaven. Another way to think of it is that heaven is restaurant. A restaurant certainly would not turn anyone away, nor will God.

Questioner: So, can I get a double cheeseburger in heaven?

Guru: You *are* the double cheeseburger. You are good and kind, are you not?

Questioner: Three arrests, no convictions.

Guru: Wonderful! Good and kind people go to heaven and get Christmas presents from Santa.

Questioner: So . . . Santa Claus is real?

Guru: You *are* Santa.

Questioner: No way.

Guru: Way. Well, I'm sorry. That's all the time I have. Be sure to visit the book table on your way out. My book *Heavenly Hash* provides celestial guidance to heaven. There's even a picture of me bungee jumping in heaven with Santa. It was great fun. Perhaps I'll tell you about it next week. So long. I'm tired and must go rest.

Announcer: Ladies and gentlemen, a big round of applause for the honorable Dr. Shaman Guru!

Almighty God, source of every blessing, your generous goodness comes to us anew every day. By the work of your Spirit lead us to acknowledge your goodness, give thanks for your benefits, and serve you in willing obedience; through your Son, Jesus Christ our Lord. Amen

Masks

Text: Luke 17:11-19 (also vv. 9-10)

Key idea: We do not have to hide from God, especially in church.

Characters: Speaker
  (This drama is a monologue.)

Setting: unspecified

Props: none

(The Speaker walks on stage, heavy in sorrow.)

Speaker: Every week it's the same old thing.
(Enthusiastically, to someone in the audience) Hey, hey, hey, hi! Hi. Hi. Hi. How's it going? How's the wife and kids? How's the job? Great! Great! Great! Me? Life's grand! Life's great! I'm blessed. God's working. God's moving. I'm a lean, mean Christian machine! Couldn't be better! Yeah, yeah, I'll see you next week. Keep smiling, brother.

(To the entire audience) It's exhausting, this show I put on! But it's good. It's impressive. It's got you fooled. Admit it. You don't really know me. See my life is divided into two parts: my public life over here and my private life over here.

In my public life I keep an impressive spiritual schedule. I got my Bible study on Monday nights, my church board meeting on Tuesday nights, I volunteer in the youth ministry on Wednesday nights, I lead a small group on Thursday nights, and on Friday I lead a prayer group. I'm a spiritual athlete.

But over here in my private life, I hide a hoard of personal defeat, inadequacies, and spiritual failure. I'm a Christian, but when I watch the horror of the nightly news I am filled with doubt. I'm an encourager to others, but underneath my breath I have an impressive vocabulary of four-letter words.

A day does not go by without the beast of greed, selfishness, and lust rearing its ugly head. I'd like to show the world this part of me, but I'm afraid if I showed you my Pandora's box of a life, you wouldn't think I was very spiritual. So, let's just keep it the way it is.

Let's keep the "Hey, hey, hey, hi! Hi. Hi. Hi. How's it going? How's the wife and kids? Great! Great! Great! Me? Life's grand! Life's great! Couldn't be better! Yeah, yeah, yeah, I'll see you next week. Keep smiling, brother."

(Exits with head hanging low.)

*Almighty God, source of every blessing, your
generous goodness comes to us anew every day.
By the work of your Spirit lead us to acknowledge
your goodness, give thanks for your benefits, and
serve you in willing obedience; through Jesus
Christ our Lord. Amen*

What about Me?

Text: Mark 10:35-45

Key idea: Selfishness plays itself out at church, too.

Characters: Elder
                        Secretary
                        Fred
                        Elise

Setting: A church sanctuary. The Elder and Church Secretary sit at a table with two microphones. The rest of the cast sits in the audience with the congregation.

Props: the Secretary needs the minutes from the last annual meeting

Note: The presentation will be funnier if the Elder and the Secretary act uncomfortable speaking in front of people.

Elder: On behalf of the leadership of First Central Church, I'd like to welcome all of you to our annual meeting. Our chair is under the weather and since I am the youngest Elder, the other Elders forced, I mean, asked me to run the meeting. Secretary, would you please read the minutes from last year's meeting.

Secretary: Certainly. *(As she reads, her mouth strays toward the written minutes more than the microphone. She does this constantly and punctuates especially dull moments with sniffs due to her hay fever.)* Am I on? Am I on? Can you hear me in the back there? Okay. The meeting was called to order by chairman Anderson at 7:03 P.M. Treasurer Lewis reported a 2 percent decrease in giving over the year leaving us unable to make our mortgage payment for November and December. Ruth Toddlemeier of the outreach team reported that attendance was up 5 percent over the first half of the year but then down 25 percent over the second half of the year, and another 30 percent over the last quarter.

Discussion ensued regarding the sudden drop in attendance. Many spirited remarks were made at Chairman Anderson followed by violent and uncalled for gestures by Chairman Anderson and his wife Marge. A motion was made and carried that the Anderson family was to blame for all of the church's woes. The motion was followed by more violent and uncalled for gestures by the Anderson children, young Hope and little Charity. A scuffle ensued. The ambulance arrived at 11:05 P.M. with chairman Anderson conceding defeat once the paramedics stopped the bleeding.

Elder Herb Frazee then took over the meeting calling for an end to communism as we know it. Tim Blau then moved that we excommunicate all the men with earrings in our fight against communism. The motion was seconded and approved. The Lewis boys, earrings in place, then stood up and made some more violent and uncalled for gestures. Another scuffle ensued with the Lewis family coming out the clear winners. The Lewis family, the Blau family, and the Frazee family then left the church never to return. Meeting adjourned at 12:05 A.M.

Elder: Thank you. That was a spirited meeting last year, wasn't it? Well, let's look at what stands before us this evening. The first order on the agenda is the issue of our continuing decline in attendance. I'd like to open the floor for discussion on the attendance problem.

(Fred raises his hand.)

Elder: Yes, Fred.

Fred: I don't care about the attendance problem. I want to know when you're going to sing something I want to sing!

Elder: Well, Fred, I appreciate your concern, but we are not talking about that issue right now.

Fred: Well, I'll tell you why no one comes to this church. It's because people are selfish here.

Elder: Well, Fred, I think . . .

Fred: Who painted the pastor's office last month?
I'll tell you who. ME! Did anyone thank me for it?
No, sir!

Secretary: Well, since we're on that subject, what about
me? I've been secretary for three years now, and has
anyone ever thanked me. Not one!

Elder: People! People! We're straying from the topic at
hand. We were discussing the reason for our decline
in attendance. Besides, if anyone has a right to com-
plain, it's me. I've taught junior-high Sunday school
for five years, and no one has ever thanked me!

Elise: Yeah, well, what about me! I've run sound here
for three years, and all I ever hear is, "It's too loud!
It's too soft! It's too loud! It's too soft!" No one ever
thanks me!

Elder: Friends, this is horrible. We've been spending so
much time thinking about God and others that we've
neglected to honor ourselves. I'd like to entertain a
motion that we devote each Sunday during the year
to honoring the 52 people left in the church. Any
discussion?

Fred: I get to be next Sunday!

Secretary: Why you? I should be first!

Elise: If I don't get to go next Sunday, I'm leaving!

Secretary: *(rising to challenge Fred)* All you think about is yourself.

Fred: Let's take it outside, buddy.

Elise: I'll take you all on!

Elder: Meeting adjourned! Meeting adjourned!

*Almighty and everlasting God, in Christ you
have revealed your glory among the nations.
Preserve the works of your mercy, that your Church
throughout the world may persevere with steadfast
faith in the confession of your name, through
your Son, Jesus Christ our Lord. Amen*

Appendix

Pages 78-80 list the dramas in the order they appear in this book, along with their key ideas, related lectionary texts, and a suggested presentation day for each sketch.

Drama Title	Key Idea	Lectionary Text	Church Day/Year
The Unveiling p. 11	We hide behind masks of goodness, especially the church.	Matthew 9: 12-13	Sunday between June 5 and 11 inclusive (if after Trinity Sunday), Proper 5, year A
Insomnia p. 14	Shame distracts us from God's love.	Matthew 11: 16-19, 25-30	Sunday between July 3 and 9 inclusive, Proper 9, year A
The Diner p. 17	The work of the hands is the work of the Spirit.	Luke 10:38-42	Sunday between July 17 and 23 inclusive, Proper 11, year C
Voices p. 24	Christ comes to liberate us from our past.	Romans 8: 26-39	Sunday between August 7 and 13 inclusive, Proper 12, year A
I Think I'm Lost p. 27	We can't make it on our own.	Colossians 2: 6-15	Sunday between July 24 and 30 inclusive, Proper 12, year C

Drama Title	Key Idea	Lectionary Text	Church Day/Year
Checkbook Theology p. 31	How do we distinguish needs from wants? How do we put God first?	Luke 12:13-21	Sunday between July 31 and August 6 inclusive, Proper 13, year C
Perspectives p. 36	Closing ourselves to one another leaves us lonely.	Ephesians 4:25—5:2	Sunday between August 7 and 13 inclusive, Proper 14, year B
I'm Parched p. 39	Treasures on earth won't last.	Luke 12:32-40	Sunday between August 7 and 13 inclusive, Proper 14, year C
My Plans p. 43	Trust God with our life plans.	Romans 12:1-8	Sunday between August 21 and August 27, Proper 16, year A
Take My Life p. 46	Freeing ourselves for service.	Luke 13:10-17	Sunday between August 21 and August 27, Proper 16, year C
I Have Needs p. 50	Selfishness versus servanthood.	Mark 8:27-38	Sunday between September 11 and 17 inclusive, Proper 19, year B

Drama Title	Key Idea	Lectionary Text	Church Day/Year
The Gift p. 55	The generosity of God.	Luke 15: 1-10 (v. 8)	Sunday between September 11 and 17 inclusive, Proper 19, year C
Is God In? p. 59	Jesus has time for us.	Mark 10:2-16	Sunday between October 2 and 8 inclusive, Proper 22, year B
Christ Is Here to See You p. 63	Life's frantic pace can exclude Jesus.	Matthew 22: 1-14	Sunday between October 9 and 15 inclusive, Proper 23, year A
Heavenly Hash p. 67	What is heaven and how do I get there?	Mark 10:17-31	Sunday between October 9 and 15 inclusive, Proper 23, year B
Masks p. 70	We do not have to hide from God, especially in church.	Luke 17:11-19 (also vv. 9-10)	Sunday between October 9 and 15 inclusive, Proper 23, year C
What about Me? p. 73	Selfishness plays itself out at church, too.	Mark 10:35-45	Sunday between October 16 and 22 inclusive, Proper 24, year B